Economics for Beginners & Dummies

By Giovanni Rigters

© **Copyright 2021 - All rights reserved.**

The content contained within this book may not be reproduced, duplicated or transmitted without direct written permission from the author or the publisher.

Under no circumstances will any blame or legal responsibility be held against the publisher, or author, for any damages, reparation, or monetary loss due to the information contained within this book, either directly or indirectly.

Legal Notice:

This book is copyright protected. It is only for personal use. You cannot amend, distribute, sell, use, quote or paraphrase any part, or the content within this book, without the consent of the author or publisher.

Disclaimer Notice:

Please note the information contained within this document is for educational and entertainment purposes only. All effort has been executed to present accurate, up to date, reliable, complete information. No warranties of any kind are declared or implied. Readers acknowledge that the author is not engaged in the rendering of legal, financial, medical or professional advice. The content within this book has been derived from various sources. Please consult a licensed professional before attempting any techniques outlined in this book.

By reading this document, the reader agrees that under no circumstances is the author responsible for any losses, direct or indirect, that are incurred as a result of the use of the information contained within this document, including, but not limited to, errors, omissions, or inaccuracies.

Table of Contents

Introduction 5

Chapter 1: The Choices We Make 8

    Land 10

    Labor 13

    Capital 17

    Entrepreneurship 20

Chapter 2: The Economy: Four Different Systems 23

    Traditional Economy 25

    Command Economy 27

    Market Economy 31

    Mixed Economy 34

Chapter 3: Supply and Demand: Finding a Balance 36

Chapter 4: Economic Factors 44

    Economic Inflation and Deflation 47

    Economic Recession and Depression 53

Conclusion 56

References 61

Introduction

In the beginning, there were the hunters and gatherers; these early humans sustained themselves by gathering edible plants and fruits while hunting animals. Following animals is difficult; finding edible plants, shelter, and safe water is exhausting. Because of the exhaustion, among other, bigger reasons, people decided to settle, grow their own food, and eventually domesticate animals. The benefit of this arrangement is that there are more people to help each other in times of need. If one person needs a tool, they can borrow it from a neighbor. As people worked together, farmed the land, and built structures, they all were able to share in the fruits of their labors.

As these settlements began to grow, things began to get more complicated. It makes sense that working as a group, spreading the work among the members, means that people have free time, time to learn a skill. This is called specialization. That is when tasks are assigned and specific roles are allocated. Rather than everyone sharing in the labor, some people specialized in farming, others in metalwork, and others in construction. Specialization is one of the most fundamental concepts in economics. Specialization is also known as a division of labor; this is particularly helpful when it relates to the scarcity of resources. We have to remember that everything in this world has its limits.

There is only so much land, so much water, so many people. In economic terms, because these resources are finite, they become scarce. This is the benefit of specialization; it allows for greater, more efficient use of scarce resources.

How these resources are used, how labor is divided—these elements of specialization are the building blocks of the economy. The economy is a huge set of interrelated factors that influence the production and consumption of goods and services and the allocation of resources and labor. In an economy, the production and consumption of goods and services are produced to meet the needs of the people living and working in the society. People need food, shelter, education, healthcare, and defense; the rest are their wants. This balance is what drives the economy. The study of this is called economics.

Economics is the scientific examination of all of the factors that drive and influence an economy. Economists study the patterns of production and consumption, the basic transfer of wealth, and the factors that influence these things such as governmental influences (taxes, regulations, etc.), as well as how scarcity of resources influence those patterns.

This is generally broken down into two areas: macro- and microeconomics. Macroeconomics concerns itself with economies of scale on a massive level like a city, state, or country. Microeconomics deals primarily with small scale economics, that is to say, the patterns of production, consumption, and the exchange of wealth on an individual level.

Just as a country must manage its resources, a person must manage their own resources.

Chapter 1: The Choices We Make

As villages become cities, and cities become countries, the needs of the people change and grow as the populations change and grow. Understanding the scarcity of resources, economists and leaders must decide how to allocate those resources for the needs of the people.

Remember, the needs of the people are split: food, shelter, healthcare, education, and defense. Governments must decide how best to allocate their resources to meet those basic needs.

How these resources are allocated involves opportunity costs. This is best demonstrated in what is called a Production Possibilities Curve, or the Guns and Butter model. In this theoretical economy, economists assume only two products will be produced: butter (food) or guns (military spending).

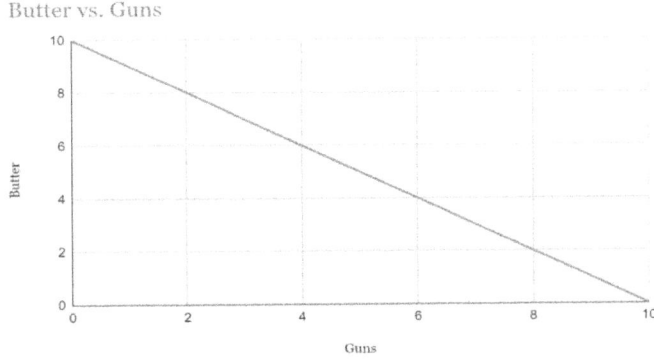

This model assumes that for every resource one allots to butter, one is taken away from guns and vice versa. The trick for decision-makers is how to balance each in order to properly support the needs of the people. If leaders allot too many resources to gun production, the people starve. If too many resources are allotted to food, their defenses fall behind and can be easily overrun.

If an economy is the interrelationship of activities that help to determine how resources are allocated, then, logically, there needs to be an understanding of what resources there are in order to produce these goods. These are called the factors of production. Economists generally divide the factors of production into four categories: land, labor, capital, and entrepreneurship.

Land

Economists define land as all the naturally occurring resources available in an area. This included actual land, lumber, water, mineral deposits, fish stocks, and even atmospheric qualities.

If we consider that everything is finite (i.e., it has limits), how land resources are allocated becomes particularly important. Consider the importance of water—without it everything dies. Water is necessary for the care of crops, animals, and people. Water is also necessary to cool the engines of military vehicles. A growing population needs to be fed and needs to be defended against potential invading forces. In this example, which is more important?

Water is required for both to survive. Perhaps in allocating resources, a synthetic coolant could be discovered and used to cool the engines of military vehicles. In this case, more water could be allocated to humanitarian needs rather than military needs. Even in humanitarian uses, the allocation of water must be divided again; allotments for drops, human and animal consumption, and even bathing must be considered.

Leaders must determine priorities and distribute the water fairly. In areas where water is scarce, like a desert, the division of water rights is of the utmost importance. Frequently, communities along a river system will argue and negotiate the allotment of water from the river system.

The animosity among communities, especially when referring to water rights, is evident today. Most recently, the state of Texas sued the state of New Mexico in the US Supreme Court (Texas v New Mexico, 2020). In the case, the state of Texas claimed that New Mexico owed the state additional water allotments to make up for water that had evaporated while being stored in a New Mexico reservoir. A tropical storm had caused Texas's Pecos River Valley to flood. In order to prevent more damages, the state asked New Mexico to slow the release of their water allotment from the Pecos River.

When stored in an open reservoir in the middle of the desert, naturally, water evaporates. The longer the water sits in the reservoir, logically, the more it evaporates. New Mexico argued that the state did as requested; they held the flow of water at the request of Texas to prevent even more flooding damage. It was not the state's fault that the Texas allotment evaporated.

Texas did not persuade the court that the water that evaporated was not, in fact, their water; it was New Mexico's water that evaporated. In the end, seven of the nine justices ruled on behalf of New Mexico, Justice Alito submitted a split decision, and Justice Barrett recused herself from the case.

Labor

Now that resources have been allotted, something has to be done with them. This is called labor. Economists describe labor as the actual manpower it takes to produce a good or service. The production of any good is a vast, interconnected chain of tasks. Consider the process needed to produce a simple hamburger.

In labor economics, the division of labor suggests that in order to produce a hamburger, individual tasks would be assigned to various specialists. First, farmers and ranchers are responsible for producing the beef and the produce (flour for wheat, vegetables, etc.). Once the basics of the hamburger have been produced, the cattle and produce are turned over to the processors to finish the next step of the process. In this step, specialists slaughter the cattle and produce ground beef, or prepare the flour and produce for the market. In this example, the division of labor is split three ways: farmer to factory, factory to market, and market to table.

Most economies rely on a division of labor built on skills. In general, labor resources are split into three sectors: unskilled, semi-skilled, and skilled laborers.

Unskilled labor refers to workers who possess no particular skill. Tasks that require unskilled workers are usually menial laborers: maids, fast food workers, janitors, grocery clerks, etc. These are jobs that don't require much skill, just the ability to perform the same task over and over again. Unfortunately for many in this category, it is becoming a smaller and smaller viable option as technology advances and the need for skilled laborers grows.

Semi-skilled labor doesn't require any type of advanced training for specialized skills, however, some skill is necessary. Semi-skilled laborers do not generally need a college education; rather, a high school diploma is usually enough. The skills necessary for semi-skilled work are usually complex, but they do require an ability to monitor and perform repetitive tasks. Retail workers, truck drivers, security guards, and taxi/uber drivers are generally considered semi-skilled jobs.

Finally, economists classify the most specialized form of labor as skilled-labor. Skilled laborers are required to have some set of specialized skills. Most likely, they are the jobs that require a college degree or a specialized certificate.

A few examples of skilled laborers are law enforcement, electricians, plumbers, financial officers, and even some sales representatives who require a specialized set of skills. Doctors, lawyers, and teachers are generally placed in a separate category within skilled labor called professionals, because they require a college degree and additional training beyond their initial, basic education.

While division of labor is considered a good thing (specialization does make for a more efficient process), one has to be concerned with overspecialization. Being over-specialized limits the amount of labor or product that can be produced.

Furthermore, as technology evolves, the need for unskilled and semi-skilled laborers declines. A visit to a local McDonald's demonstrates this principle. Traditionally, when one visits a McDonald's, they go to the counter and place their order with a person working behind the counter working the register.

As technology has improved and the use of credit and debit cards becomes more widespread, places like McDonald's no longer need to hire counter staff. Instead, the counter staff has been replaced with a touch-screen computer kiosk and a credit card reader.

Capital

Capital, in economics, is most commonly associated with money, but it also includes human capital. In this definition, human capital is the number of people in a group with the skills deemed to be of value in a population. Human capital is an intangible asset.

It is the skills a company needs based on experience, education, and training. In general, the more a company or government invests in the education of its employees or people, the more productive and successful they are.

In terms of money, capital is used to describe the financial assets of a company or government. This can be cash on hand (liquid assets) or investments and money derived from other financial sources (loans, bonds, etc). Capital can also be assessed through a company's assets: investments, property, equipment, etc.

While these assets, buildings, machinery, etc., may be fixed, they can also be sold or exchanged to add to a company's or government's liquid assets. Put simply, capital is a measurement of wealth and also a resource that can increase wealth through investments or projects (Hargrave, 2020).

When economists study financial capital, they break it into four different types. Debt capital is when a business borrows money. Sources of this capital can be friends or family, banks or investors, credit card companies, or governmental loans.

Debt capital requires a regular repayment plan with interest. That is how banks make money—they charge a little extra for every dollar that is borrowed. For example, assume an individual were to borrow $100 from the bank at a rate of 10% interest. This would mean that the individual would have to pay the bank back $110—the initial loan plus the interest charged.

Equity capital comes in three forms: public, private, and real estate equity. Private and public equity usually occur in the form of shares of a company. In order to raise money, a company may choose to sell off smaller parts, or shares, of the company.

In exchange, when the company makes a profit, shareholders are paid a small share of the profits depending on how many shares they own. Real estate equity, on the other hand, is the difference between the market value of a property and how much money is owed on the mortgage. For example, if a person has a home valued at $100,000, but only owes $65,000, the equity would be $35,000.

Finally, time can be considered a form of capital. Time is finite, and, eventually, it runs out. The world works on a schedule; there is a time to plant and a time to harvest, a time to work, and a time to sleep. Economists, leaders, and businesses must understand how fleeting time is; the wrong decisions could starve a population or cause a company to go bankrupt.

Entrepreneurship

An entrepreneur is one of the most important resources and a main drivers of economic growth. An entrepreneur is a risk-taker. An entrepreneur is a person who takes an idea or a product and turns it into a business. The survival of any economic system relies on the desire of people to create a product, to develop a plan that is new, and to innovate in a way that will stand the test of time. Being a businessperson, starting from nothing and building something, is a risky affair. Roughly 90% of all startup businesses failed to survive past the first year in 2020 (Chernev, 2020). So why do it? Well, entrepreneurs are one of the major driving factors of any economy.

Entrepreneurs play a key role in the growth of an economy. By using their skill and initiatives, entrepreneurs work to anticipate the needs of the people and bring good, new ideas and products to market to meet those needs. When one starts a business and grows it, they become job creators.

An economic system relies on the production and consumption of goods. When a business employs a worker they make an exchange; the worker performs their job in exchange for a paycheck.

When people begin earning money, they begin building wealth; that is, they increase their economic value. People with money spend it— we need food, shelter, education, and defense. In most economic systems, education and defense are provided by the government, therefore, people first spend money on food and shelter.

The rest of the purchases people make are 'wants' (wants are those things that people buy that aren't necessary for basic survival; no one needs a Sony PlayStation). As people spend their money to purchase their needs and wants, they return to the entrepreneur who reinvests it into their business in order to expand, hire more workers, and improve their product or create new ones.

This cycle is one of the primary driving forces of any economy. When products and services aren't consumed, the economy shrinks; when products and services are consumed, the economy grows.

Chapter 2: The Economy: Four Different Systems

An economy is a massive system of interrelated activities that help determine how scarce resources are used to produce and consume goods and services; there has to be a way to organize the system. In early civilizations, this wasn't that difficult as all labor was shared equally among all members.

There was a division of labor, however, it wasn't in terms of specialization. Labor was divided between household chores versus farming and hunting. In some of these early societies, women were assigned domestic work and farming while men were responsible for hunting and building shelters. Over time, these simple, small groups grew into large population centers and then countries and people began to specialize. When this happens, a traditional economy is no longer possible to maintain.

When economists and leaders work to allocate resources to provide for the needs of the people, they fall into one of four systems: traditional, command, mixed, or market economies. It is important to understand that no one, single model will work for every country, just as every financial decision won't work for every family or individual.

While there is some overlap in economic models, economists generally only recognize four economic systems.

Traditional Economy

A traditional economic system is the most basic and oldest form of an economy. Traditional economies design their economic affairs around the way it has always been done (i.e., tradition). Usually, occupations stay in the family.

This means that the work required is spread among the family or tribal unit. In this model, most families are farmers who grow traditional crops using traditional methods, because that is how it has always been done. Traditionally, this system is used among societies that rely on subsistence farming.

In this model, people consume only what they produce. If there is anything left after personal consumption (i.e., surplus), that is generally traded for other goods or services. In this system, there is no exchange of cash between producer and consumer.

One of the major drawbacks to a traditional economy is a lack of economic process or development. Another downside to this model is that it is dependent on the weather. If the crops don't grow or are destroyed by fire or another natural disaster, or if the hunt is unsuccessful and the hunters fail to provide meat, people starve.

Further, as more advanced economies grow and expand, the effects are often negative for traditionalists as the demand for natural resources increases. For example, in Russia, oil development and drilling in Siberia has polluted streams, depleted fish stocks, and limited areas for reindeer herding. This has left the traditional, nomadic people with fewer resources than they need to survive.

Traditional economies still exist today among various people across the globe. Indigenous people living in North and South America, as well as along the Arctic circle, still rely on hunting and fishing to survive.

One major factor shared among traditional economies is the geographic area in which people live. For example, Haiti is mountainous and the land is very difficult to develop. The majority of the population relies on subsistence farming and bartering (trading goods for other goods) as the primary means of survival.

Command Economy

A command, or planned economy is one in which the government determines how resources are allocated, what goods should be produced, and how much should be produced. The government also establishes how the goods will be distributed and at what price the goods will be offered for sale. The government is able to determine these things because the government owns or controls the means of production. Private ownership of land, labor, or capital is forbidden or tightly controlled for use in support of the central government's economic plan.

In a pure command economy, there is no sense of competition because the government controls or owns all businesses. This particular model relies on the collective efforts of everyone within the society to work towards a centralized, government-set goal for production.

In a command economy, governmental leaders and economists set the national economic priority. This includes determining how and when to grow the economy and how to allocate the resources of production in order to best meet the needs of the people.

In order to plan for this, most command economies implement some type of a multi-year plan that includes the entire span of the economy. The former Union of Soviet Socialistic Republics (USSR) is perhaps the best example of a five-year plan. After serving in the Russian Civil War (Bolshevik Revolution), Stalin took power after the death of Vladimir Lenin. Stalin's five-year plan was adopted in 1928 with the goal of modernizing and industrializing the former Soviet Union. In order to do this, Stalin called for a 250% increase in industrial development overall and nationalized all industry and services; managers were given quotas predetermined by the central planners, and unions were converted into mechanisms for increasing the productivity of the people (Library of Congress, 2016).

Stalin also took control of the Russian agricultural industry turning small family farms into a system of large, state-owned, collective farms. The idea was that larger, collective farms would be more efficient and produce more food to feed a growing population. This proved to be disastrous. By 1932, reports of famine and starvation began to filter its way to Russian leaders.

When economic power is consolidated in the hands of a central power with an absence of a market and competition, command economies face two major problems. The first problem is a lack of knowledge and calculation on the part of the economic planners. Every good and service produced in the economy must be calculated by the planners, including every means of production and delivery. Planners cannot predict everything that will happen in the future. For example, long term drought has a negative effect on the production of food. Failure to plan for this and set aside a stockpile of food will lead to the starvation of the people. Further, command economies provide very little to no incentives for workers to improve and perform better and more efficiently.

Because pay and wages are controlled by the government, profit is eliminated from its incentivizing role; there is no reason for workers to be efficient.

Also, because the government controls prices and profits, there is no incentive to improve current products. Consider the advent of the cell phone. Every year the major cell phone makers (Apple, Samsung, LG, etc.) release new phone models. With each year, the technology gets better, the process to produce the phone becomes more efficient, and profits from each cell phone sold go back to the company that produced it.

In this example, the ability to make a profit is the draw to improve the cell phone every year. In a command system, the incentive to make money is removed and worker motivation declines.

The Democratic Peoples' Republic of Korea (aka. North Korea) operates a command economy. In North Korea, the Supreme Commander has complete control over the allocation of resources, production of goods, and consumption.

Currently, the Supreme Commander has chosen to allocate most of the country's resources on defense needs leaving little for humanitarian needs (recall the Guns and Butter model.

While Kim Jung-Un displays the country's massive weaponry on parade, the people in the countryside starve. Underground economies (i.e., black markets) flourish under a command system as people try to provide for their needs and wants outside of the government's approval.

Market Economy

If a command economy is one in which the state controls the means of production, sets prices, and controls the allocation of resources, a market economy is the exact opposite. In a purely free market (i.e., capitalist) economy, the government takes a laissez-faire, or hands-off, approach to the allocation of resources, production, and consumption of goods and services, allowing the market to regulate itself.

In a market economy, the government does little-to-nothing to regulate resources, control production or prices, nor does the government regulate a basic minimum wage employers must pay their employees.

In a market economy, consumers and the desire for profit dictate the cost of goods and services and the wages of workers. A business in this model would set prices as high as their consumers will pay and set wages as low as an employee would accept. In this model, profit drives all commerce forcing businesses to work as efficiently as possible to maximize profit and avoid losing customers to the competition.

By the same token, if consumers aren't buying a product or the market is flooded with it, a business must make adjustments or, between low profits and high expenses (materials, employees, etc.), that business will fail, leaving a product gap in the market and many, many people unemployed.

Mixed Economy

A mixed is the most widely used system in the world. A mixed economy combines elements of both command and market economies. While a market economy brings buyers and sellers together, a mixed economy allows for some government control in order to provide for the defense and various needs of the people.

Many European nations allow for free market trade, however, some aspects of the economy such as healthcare and education are controlled by the state. The United States is another example of a mixed market system that leans more towards a market economy system. The

United States leaves most of the economic decisions to the buyer and seller, however, there are some products and industries that are highly regulated. For example, the US government regulates various aspects of the agricultural market.

In order to maintain an even price on staple food items like milk, the government regulates how much milk is produced for the market. The government does the same with corn and sugar. The idea behind the regulation is to keep the prices of these items at a relatively stable price with minimal fluctuation.

China and Russia, both long time command economies, have begun to open to a market-based economy. While these countries have allowed for some market economy privatization of land and resources, the government maintains control over most aspects of the decision-making process. While many Chinese companies are still owned by the state, the government has allowed western companies and investors to enter the Chinese markets.

Chapter 3: Supply and Demand: Finding a Balance

Wandering through the grocery store in the produce aisle, there are two bins full of pink lady apples. One bin of apples is marked $1.50 a pound and the other is marked $2.25 a pound. Both bins are full of the same type of apple, so where is there a .$75 difference in price?

The more expensive bin is marked 'organic.' As the popularity for organic foods has exploded worldwide, organic foods have become a mainstream item in most grocery stores today. Organic farming is, by its nature, slow. Because organic food uses no pesticides, most orchards are small so that no apples are wasted. Further, in organic food, genetically modified plants are unacceptable; the apple trees don't grow as much fruit, and they are more susceptible to different fungi and tree diseases. Because of these factors, organic pink lady apple orchards do not produce as many apples as a large commercial orchard.

Given the large numbers of customers wanting organic apples and the short supply, organic apple farmers can charge as much as the market will bear for their apples. This, in economics, is called the law of supply and demand.

The law of supply and demand demonstrates that the relationship between a product and consumer is in direct opposition. When the demand for a product is high and the supply is low, the price for that product is high.

Conversely, if the demand for a product is low, the price for that product will also be low. At an imaginary auction, a bidder pays $10,000 for a dress worn by Marilyn Monroe. While some would look at this as a waste of money, to a collector, this is a rare, desirable item well worth the money paid out.

In economics, the law of supply and demand is based on three concepts: supply, demand, and equilibrium. Supply is defined as anything that can be produced for consumer purchase. This can include raw materials such as minerals and lumber to finished goods like the Sony PlayStation or an automobile. Demand is a fairly simple concept.

In this sense, demand is the amount of goods or services consumers are willing to purchase at the set price. Demand is based on needs and wants, and, while a consumer may be able to differentiate between the two, economists view needs and wants as the same thing.

Further, demand for a product is also based on the ability to pay for it—if one cannot afford a product, they have no real demand for it. The cost of a specific good or service is called price. A fall in price will always create more demand as more people can afford goods or services offered. On the other hand, a rise in price will almost always result in a loss of demand as people look for ways to reduce their consumption of goods and services.

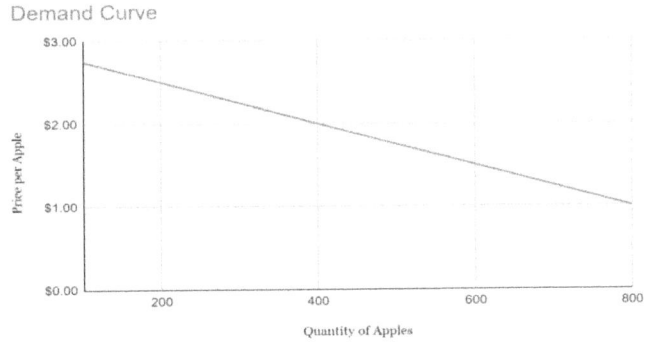

The table above is known as a demand curve. A demand curve is a visual representation of the correlation between supply and demand. In this example, the price per apple is represented on the vertical axis; the number (quantity) of apples harvested is represented on the horizontal axis. Clearly, as the number of apples available increases, the price of the apple decreases. With only 200 apples harvested, the price per apple is $2.50, however, when 800 apples are harvested, the price per apple falls to just $1.00.

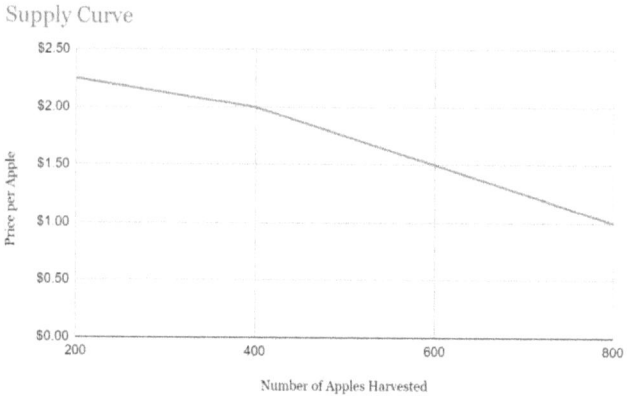

Economists use a supply curve to demonstrate the relationship between price and supply levels. In the above supply curve, the price per apple is shown on the vertical axis and the number of apples harvested is demonstrated along the horizontal axis.

When supply is low, the cost for a product increases. Conversely, as a company produces more products (apples, for example), the price of the product falls. In the above supply curve, consumers pay $2.25 per apple because of the limited quantity produced, 200 in this model. As more apples are produced, the price per apple drops.

Following the trend line in the supply chart, the price per apple falls to $1.50 once producers have harvested 600 apples.

The trick for any business or economy is to find equilibrium. Equilibrium is the balance between supply and demand; it is the price where the plans of the consumer and the plans of the producer agree. In other words, equilibrium is when the amount of the product consumers want to buy is equal to the amount producers want to sell. Economists combine both the supply chart and the demand chart to determine the point of equilibrium.

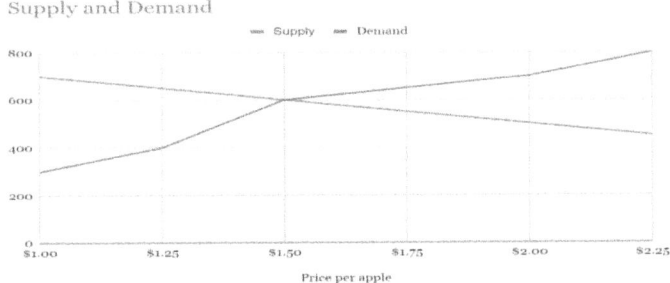

In this case, when the demand for apples and the supply of apples reach equilibrium, the cost of an apple is $1.50.

The limit of the supply and demand curves is that it only demonstrates the relationship between two variables: the quantity of products produced and the price of the product. In product and supply depend on more factors than just price. For example, a consumer's demand for a product depends on their income and a producer's supply depends on the cost of producing the product. When a restaurant owner sets the prices for their menu, they factor in the cost of all of the ingredients in a dish. If the cost of beef increases, then the restaurant owner must also increase the price of the burger in order to maintain their profit margin (that is the difference between what a business earned in income minus the cost of production).

Similarly, if a consumer experiences a loss or reduction of income, they will be unable to purchase high end (i.e., expensive) goods.

Economists must also include changing tastes and preferences of the population. As populations change, so do their buying preferences. The American automotive industry is a prime example of this phenomenon. For the first time in 2015, sales of sport utility vehicles (SUV) outpaced the sales of sedans (Voelk, 2021).

This shift in sales was the result of changing tastes among American car buyers. Buyers preferred the practicality and ride height of the SUV. They are considered more functional and more visible than a sedan and, thus, more appealing to American car buyers.

Business owners and economists alike also study changes in the composition of the population to explain changes in the supply and demand of products. As populations age, there is a higher demand for assisted living facilities and hearing aids. Similarly, a younger population will have a greater demand for goods and services like daycare centers and nightlife venues.

It isn't just age shifts in population that affect goods and services. Grocery stores in ethnic neighborhoods are more likely to stock foodstuff more familiar to the surrounding community. For example, in a largely Hispanic neighborhood, the local market is more likely to stock more Hispanic foods than Asian food.

Additionally, many goods are complements for each other and are often used together. For example, notebooks and pens, golf balls and golf clubs, hypercars and high-end gasoline are all complementary products. If the price of golf clubs rise due to a fall in the demand for them (law of supply and demand), then the cost of golf balls would also increase.

Chapter 4: Economic Factors

Nothing in the world of economics just happens; it is always a cause and effect relationship. If there is a change on the supply side of production, it will affect the price point on consumer goods.

If the cost of production decreases, then, theoretically, the consumer cost should also decrease (or the profit margin for the producer will increase if the changes to the consumer price isn't adjusted equally). Similarly, if the cost of production increases, then the consumer cost of the product will also increase.

In addition to the cost of production and the tastes of consumers, economies are affected by nearly every decision governments, financial institutions, and individuals make. Depending on the style of the economy (command, market, or mixed), governmental intervention is one of the largest factors that affect a nation's economy.

Governments have the ability to levy taxes on goods and services, as well as income for both companies and individuals. Some of these taxes are meant to provide for the needs of the people while others are meant to act as a deterrent for risky behaviors. For example, most taxes collected in the United States are used to fund social programs like healthcare for seniors and indigent (i.e., poor) populations, defense needs, and education.

Similarly, governments may impose a tax to shift consumer behaviors like smoking tobacco. Various states in the United States serve as examples for levying taxes for this reason. In an effort to limit the health issues associated with smoking, many states have implemented a "sin tax."

The average price of a pack of cigarettes is around $1.50 per pack of 20 cigarettes in 2016 (Cammenga, 2019). The federal government levies a $1.00 tax, and states and cities will add on to that as well; what began as a $1.50 pack of cigarettes will now cost a consumer well over $8.00 a pack depending on what state the cigarettes are bought.

It is well known that smoking is harmful to one's health. By driving up the cost of a pack of cigarettes with taxes, the result is that it makes cigarettes prohibitively expensive for many consumers while others will give up the habit just because they no longer want to pay exorbitant amounts of money for cigarettes. At issue for the government is that as fewer people pick up smoking, cigarette tax revenue is no longer a reliable source of income.

Governments may intervene in the economy in order to address inequity issues. In mixed or market economies, there is likely to be inequality and poverty. This is not necessarily due to merit, but it could be due to advantages some may have over others (e.g., inherited wealth or access to superior education).

Governments will generally intervene to provide some sort of basic security net for the people. This comes in the form of unemployment benefits, minimum income for the sick and disabled, free public education, and healthcare.

For example, a government may regulate the price of basic food items in order to prevent wild fluctuations of price so that even the sick and disabled receiving a minimum income can still buy food.

Among the duties of a government is to provide for the welfare of the population. For this to happen, the government must intervene in the economy through regulations. While command economies are controlled by the state, market and mixed economies apply some regulations on economic participation. For example, in the

United States, the federal government demands that most employers must compensate their employees with a minimum hourly wage. This to prevent employers from exploiting desperate and uneducated workers.

In theory, a minimum wage should provide enough income to allow individuals to provide food, shelter, and clothing for themselves. Further, in order to protect the youth of the population, some countries have implemented child labor laws. These laws are designed to protect children from being forced into labor and exploited by their employers. In the United States, for example, the minimum age to hold a job without a special permit is 16 years old.

Economic Inflation and Deflation

Briefly, inflation is an increase in the prices of goods and services throughout a sustained period of time. In other words, inflation is the measurement of the rate of rising prices of goods and services in an economic system. A surge in demand for products or services can be a cause of inflation as buyers are willing to pay more for a product. The rarer an item is, the more inflated the price of that item is. For example, consider the price of a diamond. Considered one of the hardest stones on earth, the diamond is frequently used in commercial applications as the addition to the cutting surface of a saw (i.e., a diamond-tip saw blade). Affixed to a saw blade, a diamond isn't that expensive.

However, a diamond ring will cost some money. Among diamonds used for jewelry, they tend to be more expensive as the quality of the stone is greater than those used for saw blades. The better quality the stone, the more expensive it is.

It should be noted that inflation is expressed as a percentage rate. So if inflation is 2% per year, a gallon of milk that was $3.00 a year ago will now cost $3.06.

Inflation can be a sign of a growing economy. When an economy expands, unemployment drops and wages generally rise. As the demand for goods increases, businesses hire more workers. This means that more people are working and earning money.

When people have money, they spend it. The more money people earn, the more willing they are to buy both basic needs and luxury items.

The higher demand allows suppliers and producers to increase their profits, which leads to more jobs and puts money back into the economy. In this case, inflation is positive for the economy as long as the growth of inflation stays at a relatively low rate. The Federal Reserve wants there to be inflation, as it is the sign of a growing economy. That said, the Federal Reserve prefers a low inflation rate between 2%-3% annually.

Another cause of inflation is an injection of money into the economy. This happens when the government prints money at a higher rate than the growth of the economy or when the central bank (i.e., the Federal Reserve) lowers the interest rates on loans. With more money in circulation, the value of it declines and prices go up.

Injecting cash into the economy or lowering interest rates does spur people to spend money and grow the economy, however, it is risky. If interest rates are too low for too long or the central bank injects too much cash into the system, it can lead to hyperinflation. When the prices for goods and services soar to over 50% in one month, economists call this hyperinflation.

Government regulations are yet another way to inflate the economy. These usually come in the form of tariffs. Simply put, a tariff is a tax placed on goods being imported or exported from one nation to another.

They are usually paid to the country in which a product is imported and are intended to protect similar products produced in the same country a foreign good is being imported to. Most often the cost of the tariff is passed onto the consumer.

At its worst, inflation lowers the value of currency. As a result, the cost of goods and services increases. This in turn sets off a decline in the purchasing power of money (it takes more money to purchase fewer things), which results in less consumer spending. Less consumer spending leads to businesses cutting back on investing and spending, and some results in laying off workers.

Unemployed workers, in turn, don't have money to spend like they did when they were employees, causing businesses to let even more people go and eventually go out of business altogether. However, before the worst happens, central banks may combat inflation by taking cash out of the economy and increasing interest rates. By doing this, the bank is able to slow the economy before it teeters on disaster and collapses.

If inflation is a loss in purchasing power, then deflation is when consumer and asset prices decrease over time and purchasing power increases. If left unchecked and deflation is exacerbated, it can put the economy in a spiral. Deflation happens when decreases in price lead to lower production, which, in turn, leads to lower wages. Lower wages then lead to lower demand for goods and services by consumers and businesses, which only leads to further decreases in prices.

Most economists believe that there are two major causes of deflation. Deflation can be caused by an overall decline in demand for a product or service. This can happen for several reasons. A decline in the money supply or an increase in interest rates on loans leads to higher borrowing costs which discourage people and businesses from spending.

Another cause of deflation and a decline in demand is caused by a decline in consumer confidence in the market. When the economy is in decline, in a recession for example, people become more pessimistic about the future success and growth of the economy. Needless to say, when this happens people prefer to increase their savings and reduce their current spending habits.

An increase in the overall supply is another cause of inflation. When this happens, because the cost to make a product is substantially lower due to the surplus supply, other businesses are able to enter into the market with similar products. The growth of supply can be caused by several factors.

A decline in production costs is another cause of deflation. A decline in price for production inputs (e.g., oil) will lower production costs. Lower production costs mean that businesses will be able to increase their production output which will lead to an oversupply in the economy. If the demand for the product remains unchanged or declines, producers will need to lower their prices to keep consumers buying them.

Advances in technology are another possible cause of deflation. As technology advances, it makes the process of production more efficient. This, in turn, causes an increase in aggregate supply. Technological advances allow producers to lower costs.

While the concept of deflation sounds advantageous, causing an increase of production and prices and increased consumer power, deflation, if left unchecked, can harm an economy. Because producers are forced to decrease the price of their products, deflation leads to a rise in unemployment. As companies lose money selling their product, they tend to cut costs by reducing the workforce. Further, when the economy begins to deflate, interest rates on loans increase.

As a result, the cost of borrowing money becomes more expensive, making consumers less likely to apply for a loan and defer their spending until better economic days. Finally, deflation can spiral. When deflation spirals, it causes a situation where decreasing prices trigger a chain reaction. A deflation spiral leads to lower production, lower wages, decreased demand, and lower price levels. If a deflation spiral coincides with a recession, it becomes a significant challenge because it worsens the economic stability.

Economic Recession and Depression

Economies grow and shrink all of the time; they expand and contract depending on whatever outside forces are acting upon it (governmental, social, or natural). In economics, a recession and depression are, in essence, the same thing. A recession is defined as a significant decline in activity spread across the economy that lasts more a few months.

During a recession, economists observe a decline in the country's Gross National Product (GNP is the terminal value of all of the goods and services produced by a country's residents and businesses during a specific time period); usually this analysis and observation is done every year. A depression is the same decline in economic activity, however, it can last years. The Great Depression, for example, lasted over four years (1929-1933).

A recession is a point in the business cycle when economic growth peaks and then begins to reverse and the economy shrinks. Typically, economists have identified six key economic factors that, combined, indicate a country has or is about to enter a period of economic recession (Shiskin, 1974):

- The decline in gross national product for six consecutive months
- An overall decline of 1.5% of GNP

- A six-month decline in manufacturing

- A decline of 1.5% in non-farm related employment

- A reduction in jobs in more than 75% of industries for 6 months or more (this includes all industries in an economy: tourism and hospitality, manufacturing, education, service, etc.)

- A two-point rise in unemployment to a level of at least 6% of all people currently able to work

While most people view recessions as a negative, there can be some positive outcomes. Some economists argue that a recession can enable an economy to reform and to be more productive in the long term. Recessions tend to shock the system and force many inefficient firms to go out of business. However, in a recession, a new business can emerge. Beginning a business is risky at best; doing it during a recession forces business owners to be more efficient in order to survive a dismal economic situation.

Conclusion

At its heart, economics is the study of the choices people make with the resources they have. These decisions must be made at both the microeconomic (i.e., individual, family, business) level and the macroeconomic (i.e., city, state, country governments) level. All of these choices must be made with the understanding that natural resources are not infinite and must be allocated as efficiently and responsibly as possible.

Economists and those making economic decisions must understand the scarcity of resources. Natural resources are finite and, eventually, they will run out. There is only so much land and the resources that come with it (water, minerals, lumber, etc). Labor is another resource. In economics, labor refers to how tasks are assigned based on the skill level of the employee. Economists define capital as anything of value within a household, company, or government—this includes cash or fixed assets (e.g., building, machinery, labor). Finally, the ability to build a business, create a product, take an idea and turn it into a profitable endeavor, that is to say an individual's entrepreneurial ability, is one of the greatest resources people have.

In determining the allocation of resources, decision-makers must consider the needs of the people versus their wants. People need food, shelter, education, defense, and healthcare; the rest is a luxury. To better understand the effects of decisions made by the population, economists use the Production Possibilities Curve (or Guns and Butter model). The Production Possibilities Curve is a simplified visual representation of how economic decisions affect other areas of the economy. For every resource allocated to one need, that resource is removed from another need of the people.

There are four basic systems of economies. The oldest form is a traditional economy. In this system, tradition guides economic decisions; things are done in a specific way and labor is divided according to tradition. Traditional economies are found primarily in small, self-sufficient communities that rely on hunting, gathering, and agriculture for survival. Command economies are under the complete control of the government. In this system, the government owns all of the resources and means of production. North Korea is a prime example of a command economy; the state owns all of the resources and means of production. In this system, the country leader makes all of the allocation decisions. A market economy system is one in which the government takes a hands-off approach. Rather, consumers and a desire for profits control the economic decisions. Finally, most countries employ a mixed economy. A mixed economy combines aspects of market and command economies.

A mixed system allows a level of economic freedom in the capital and works to protect private property, however, this system allows for the government to interfere in order to achieve social aims. For example, in most European nations, the military, education, and healthcare are under the control of the government, however, most other economic decisions are left up to the market and consumers.

Most decisions in an economic system are based on the law of supply and demand. In economics, supply is defined by anything used to create a product and the product itself. The demand for a product is directly correlated to the supply and the willingness of individuals to pay. The law of supply and demand demonstrates that as supply increases, demand decreases, and as demand increases, supply decreases. The intersection of supply and demand is known as equilibrium. Equilibrium can be defined as the point in which the supply of a product equals the demand.

The 'economy' isn't self-sustaining and requires constant monitoring and care. Interest rates, taxes, supply and demand, labor, and wages all factor in and have an effect on the economy. Perhaps the largest factor impacting the economy is governmental activity. In order to stabilize the economy, governments regulate labor laws and wages (e.g., minimum wage).

Governments are able to inject cash into an economic system to stimulate it or withdraw cash in order to slow it down to avoid rates of inflation or deflation. Inflation is defined as a continual increase in the price of goods and services due to the devaluing of the currency. This can happen when the government adds too much cash into the system. Typically, this is done to jumpstart economic growth. On the other hand, when the government takes money out of the system, this is called deflation. Less money in the system slows economic growth and is usually implemented to counter inflation.

Wealth is a measurement of all of the assets of worth (cash, house, investments, etc.) owned by an individual, community, company, or country. Wealth is the accumulation of scarce resources measured by taking the total market value of all of the physical and intangible assets owned and then subtracting all debts. In the end, economics is about building wealth—wealth for individuals, companies, and governments.

References

AhmadArdity. (2017, July 2). *Stock Trading Financial - Free photo on Pixabay.* Pixabay.com. https://pixabay.com/photos/stock-trading-financial-finance-2463798/

Cammenga, J. (2019, April 10). *How High Are Cigarette Taxes in Your State?* Tax Foundation; Tax Foundation. https://taxfoundation.org/2019-state-cigarette-tax-rankings/

Chernev, B. (2020, November 21). *What Percentage of Startups Fail? [2020's Startup Statistics].* Review42. https://review42.com/what-percentage-of-startups-fail/

Daniel_Nebreda. (2020, March 4). *Women Work Business - Free photo on Pixabay*. Pixabay.com. https://pixabay.com/photos/women-work-business-people-market-4900849/

Fotoworkshop4You. (2016, August 2). *Market Vegetable Farmers - Free photo on Pixabay*. Pixabay.com. https://pixabay.com/photos/market-vegetable-market-1558658/

Ghinzo. (2020, May 7). *Compass Map Retro - Free photo on Pixabay*. Pixabay.com. https://pixabay.com/photos/compass-map-retro-geography-5137269/

Library of Congress. (2016). *Collectivization and Industrialization*. Loc.Gov.

https://www.loc.gov/exhibits/archives/coll.html#:~:text=Stalin's%20First%20Five%2DYear%20Plan,expansion%20in%20heavy%20industry%20alone.

Matteo Badini. (2020, March 5). *Photo by Matteo Badini on Unsplash*. Unsplash.com; Unsplash. https://unsplash.com/photos/MOt9n7clBcE

Mediator. (2020, June 13). *Coffee Coin Digital - Free photo on Pixabay*. Pixabay.com. https://pixabay.com/photos/coffee-coin-digital-cappuccino-5288659/

nattanan23. (2017, August 30). *Money Finance Business - Free photo on Pixabay*. Pixabay.com.

https://pixabay.com/photos/money-finance-business-success-2696234/

Oldani, D. (2020, May 10). *blue classic car parked on sidewalk during daytime.* Unsplash.com; Unsplash. https://unsplash.com/photos/_eh9OCAshIU

Pixabay.com. (2016). Rio Grande Water Texas National Park Desert. In *www.pixabay.com.* https://pixabay.com/photos/rio-grande-river-water-texas-1584102/

Texas v. New Mexico, (US Supreme Court December 14, 2020). https://www.supremecourt.gov/opinions/20pdf/22o65_dc8e.pdf

Rise of S.U.V.s: Leaving Cars in Their Dust, With No Signs of Slowing. (2021). *The New*

York Times. https://www.nytimes.com/2020/05/21/business/suv-sales-best-sellers.html

Shiskin, J. (1974). The Changing Business Cycle. *The New York Times.*

TLSPAMG. (2017, January 17). *Hut Lifestyle Tribal - Free photo on Pixabay.* Pixabay.com. https://pixabay.com/photos/hut-lifestyle-tribal-rural-1986886/

Tumisu. (2020, January 12). *Wall Street Stock Exchange Finance - Free photo on Pixabay.* Pixabay.com. https://pixabay.com/photos/wall-street-stock-exchange-finance-4758079/

Voelk, T. (2021). Rise of S.U.V.s: Leaving Cars in Their Dust, With No Signs of

Slowing. *The New York Times.* https://www.nytimes.com/2020/05/21/business/suv-sales-best-sellers.html

www.ingramcontent.com/pod-product-compliance
Ingram Content Group UK Ltd.
Pitfield, Milton Keynes, MK11 3LW, UK
UKHW021304180426
11947UKWH00015B/1008